What is an insect? Many people think all tiny animals that crawl are insects. They think spiders, scorpions, mites, centipedes, millipedes, crabs, and even lobsters are insects. But none of these animals is an insect. They may *look* like insects, but once you know what to look for, you will see that they are not.

One difference between insects and all other animals is the number of legs they have. In the entire animal kingdom, only insects have six legs. Another thing you can look for is the number of wings. Most adult insects have four wings, and no other animals do. Also, insects have *two antennae* (an-**ten**-ee) on their heads. These sense organs are usually located right between the eyes.

On these pages, there is only one true insect. Can you find it without reading the captions on the pictures? If you can't, don't worry. This book will help you learn how to tell the difference between insects and other animals.

MILLIPEDE

Can this be an insect? It is called a *millipede* (mil-i-peed), which means "thousand legged." Millipedes don't actually have a thousand legs, but they have too many legs to be insects.

VELVET MITE

This little animal certainly looks like an insect. But if you look closely, you will see that it has no antennae. So it cannot be an insect, because all insects have two antennae on their heads.

THAI CENTIPEDE

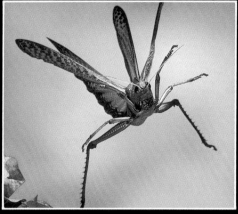

Count the number of legs on this animal. Count its wings and its antennae. You are right—this grasshopper is an insect! It has six legs, four wings, and two antennae.

People often think that spiders are insects. And at first glance, they look like insects. But they are not very closely related. For one thing, spiders have eight legs instead of six. And they don't have wings or antennae.

WOLF SPIDER

GIANT WOOD LOUSE

This little animal has many names. It is called a "sow bug," a "pill bug," and a "wood louse." It has antennae like insects do. But it isn't an insect, because it has too many antennae—and too many legs.

YELLOW SAHARAN SCORPION

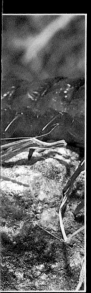

This creature has two large antennae —but it isn't an insect. It's a *centipede* (sen-ti-peed), which means "hundred legged." It is closely related to the millipede, as you may have guessed. Like the millipede, it has too many legs to be an insect.

Scorpions are close relatives of spiders. They have long, slender bodies like insects. But scorpions don't have wings or antennae. So they cannot be insects.

The body of an insect is a masterpiece of design. In many ways, insect bodies are much more efficient than our own. The basic design is quite simple. The bodies of all insects are divided into three sections, as shown at right. The sections common to all insects are the *head,* the *thorax* (**thor**-aks), and the *abdomen* (**ab**-duh-muhn).

The head has two eyes, two antennae, and a mouth. Insects eat a wide variety of food. To do this, they have a wide variety of mouth shapes. But there are really only four basic kinds of mouths. Some insects have mouths that *soak up* liquids like sponges. Others have mouths that are made for *sucking.* Many have mouths that pierce like hypodermic needles. And a large number of them use their mouths for *crushing and chewing.*

All the basic parts of an insect are easy to see on a grasshopper.

2 ANTENNAE
4 WINGS
ABDOMEN
HEAD
THORAX
6 LEGS

Flies belong to a group of insects called *diptera* (dipt-ur-uh), which means "two wings." But don't let the name fool you. They really have four wings like other insects. However, the back two are just tiny stubs that are usually hidden beneath the front wings. See if you can find the back two "wings" on this fly.

This fly has long mouth parts that end in a broad tip. The tip is porous, and the fly uses it like a sponge to soak up water and other liquids. Can you find the fly's sponging mouth parts?

GREEN BOTTLE FLY

MOSQUITO ON HUMAN ARM

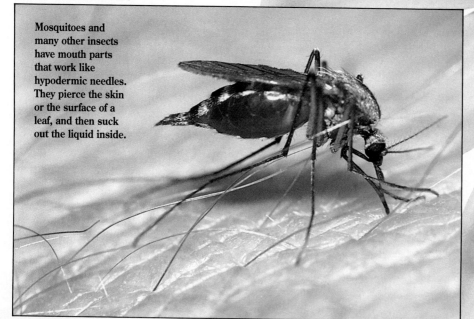

Mosquitoes and many other insects have mouth parts that work like hypodermic needles. They pierce the skin or the surface of a leaf, and then suck out the liquid inside.

Many insects have mouths that work like ours—they bite and chew. But insects don't have teeth. So they need jaws that are strong and have sharp edges to cut and chew their food. Tiger beetles move their jaws sideways to chew their food, not up and down.

4

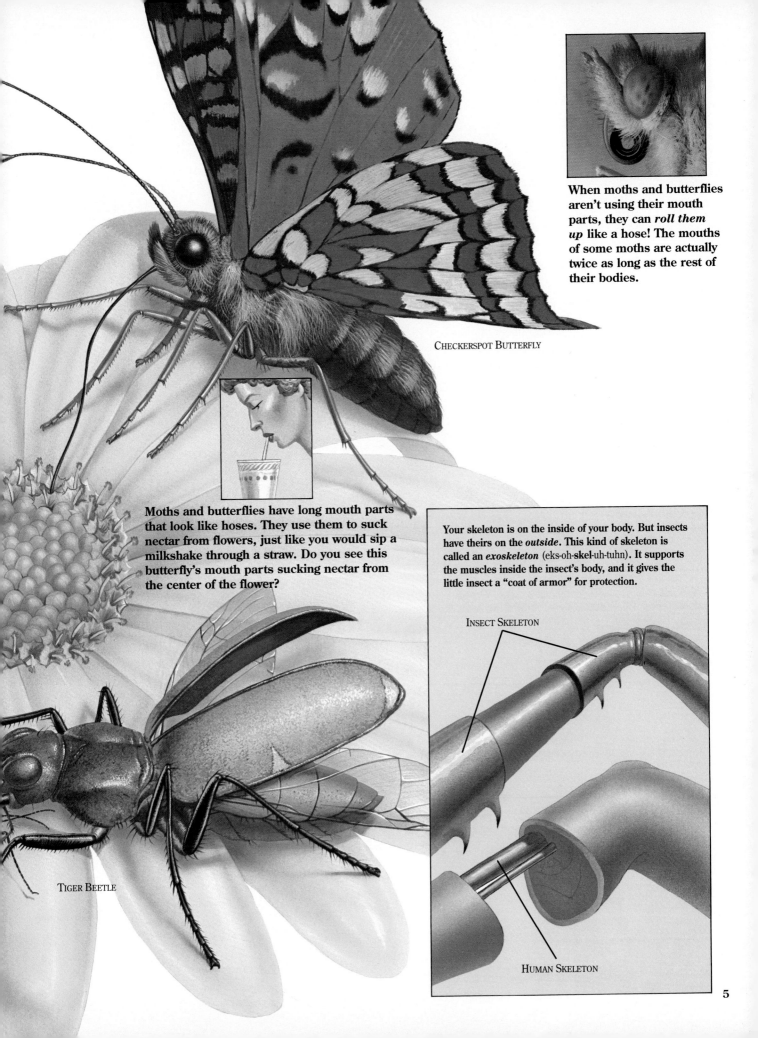

When moths and butterflies aren't using their mouth parts, they can *roll them up* like a hose! The mouths of some moths are actually twice as long as the rest of their bodies.

CHECKERSPOT BUTTERFLY

Moths and butterflies have long mouth parts that look like hoses. They use them to suck nectar from flowers, just like you would sip a milkshake through a straw. Do you see this butterfly's mouth parts sucking nectar from the center of the flower?

TIGER BEETLE

Your skeleton is on the inside of your body. But insects have theirs on the *outside*. This kind of skeleton is called an *exoskeleton* (eks-oh-skel-uh-tuhn). It supports the muscles inside the insect's body, and it gives the little insect a "coat of armor" for protection.

INSECT SKELETON

HUMAN SKELETON

5

A spectacular variety of shapes has developed out of the basic insect design. All three sections of the body can grow into very strange forms. In general, the weird bodies of insects help them to survive in one way or another.

The bodies of many insects are made for hiding. Some hide and wait to ambush their prey. Others hide to keep predators from finding them. An insect may escape from predators because it looks like part of a tree, plant, or flower.

Some insects want to be seen. Their bodies may look scary to keep predators away. Others have "horns" that can be used for fighting with other insects. Some have stingers they can use for defense or for killing their prey. And many insects have hard "shells" that protect them like armor.

This beetle uses its exoskeleton like a turtle uses its shell. If it is attacked, it simply hides under its "shell." It has large feet that can grip leaves or stems with incredible strength. When predators can't pull the beetle over, they give up and go away.

TORTOISE BEETLE

NORTH AMERICAN TREEHOPPER

This insect looks like it's made of dead leaves and sticks. This makes it hard to see when it hides among real leaves and sticks—so predators are less likely to find it.

The prize for "weirdest-looking insects" goes to the treehoppers. They all have odd formations on their backs. The one shown above looks like a thorn. The one below looks like it came from another planet. Scientists are not sure why it is shaped this way.

LARVA OF AUSTRALIAN WALKING STICK

SOUTH AMERICAN TREEHOPPER

Make a Bug Mobile

Materials: Construction paper, scissors, chalk, string, 2 plastic straws

1. Take another look at the insects in this book. Choose several for your bug mobile.

2. Cut your insect shapes out of colored paper. Add details with felt pens. Or cut insect shapes out of this book and mount them on paper.

3. Tie your finished insects to the straws with string. You may need to slide the insects back and forth on the straws until the mobile is in balance.

🦋 Hang your bug mobile in your room.

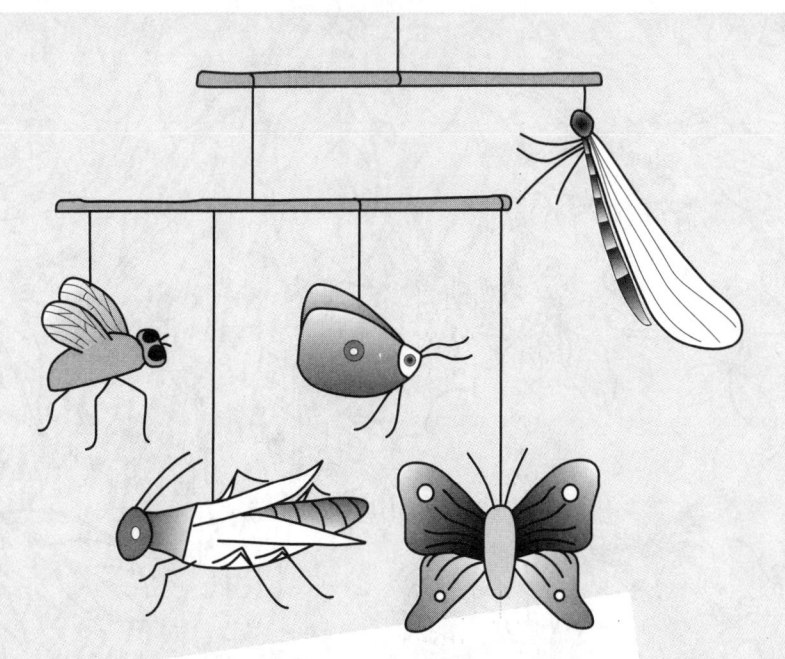

B Is for Bright Colors

Insects can be quite beautiful. Some even come in bright colors. Use your crayons or felt pens to make these insects come alive with color. Use the code below to make the insects look true to life. *Find more colorful insects on pages 16 and 17.*

B = Black   Y = Yellow   R = Red   O = Orange

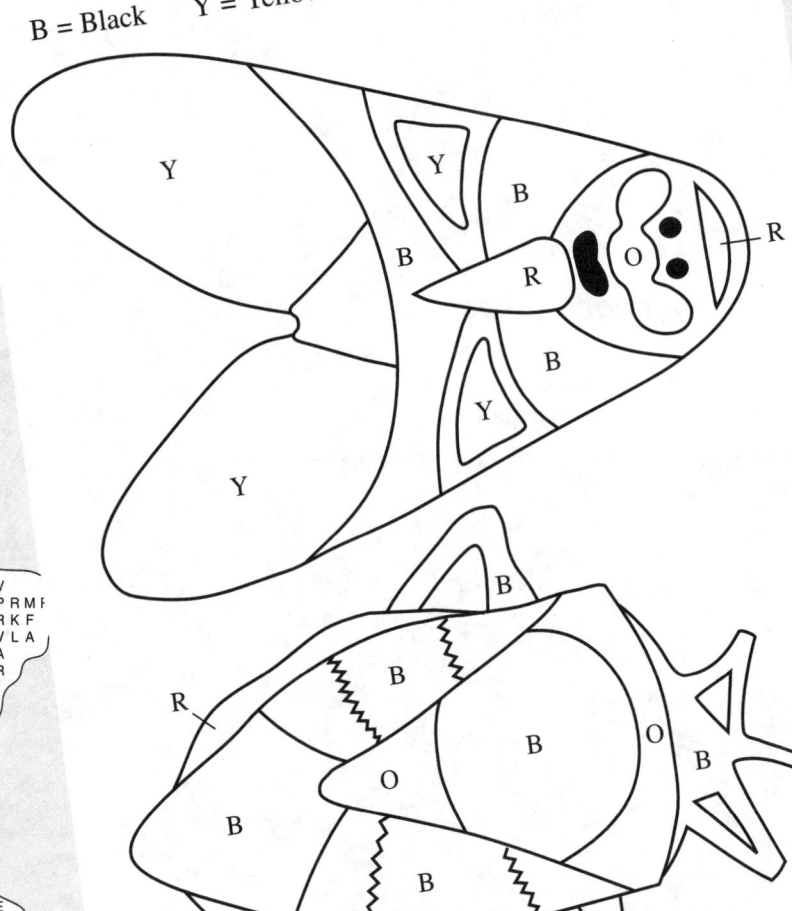

Answer Key

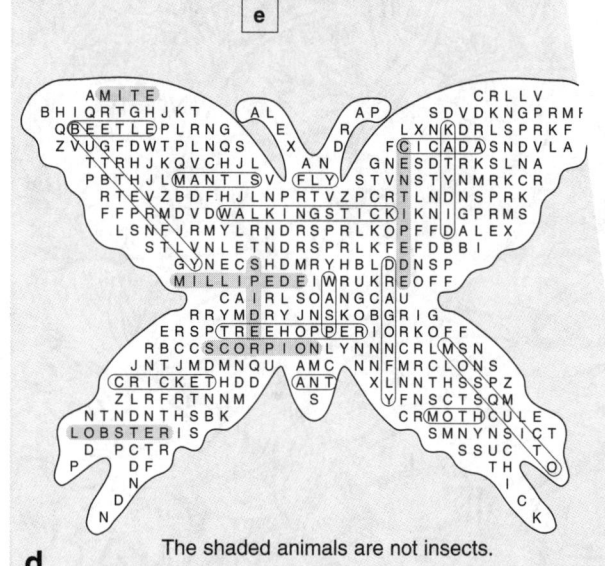

The shaded animals are not insects.

d

Parents, try these activities with your young children:

🦋 Ask questions about the pictures in this issue. For example, "What do you see?" "What is happening here?" "What do you think it would be like to be a butterfly?"

🦋 Count together to see how many insects are in this book. (We found more than 50.)

🦋 Discuss how insects move based on the pictures in this issue. Then act out the movements of different insects.

🦋 Ask, "Which is your favorite insect picture? Why?" Invite your child to draw pictures of insects. Encourage your child's creativity and don't be too critical of the results.

🦋 Make torn-paper insects out of colored paper. Tear the paper into the shape of an insect (get ideas from pictures in this book). Remember, your child might make one that only he or she can recognize as an insect.

Camouflaged Insects

Can you find the 25 insects hiding in the picture on this page? *Read about camouflage on page 16.*

A Mazing Insects

Help each insect find its way through the maze. Match each insect with the picture that shows how it moves. *For help, turn to pages 10 and 11.*

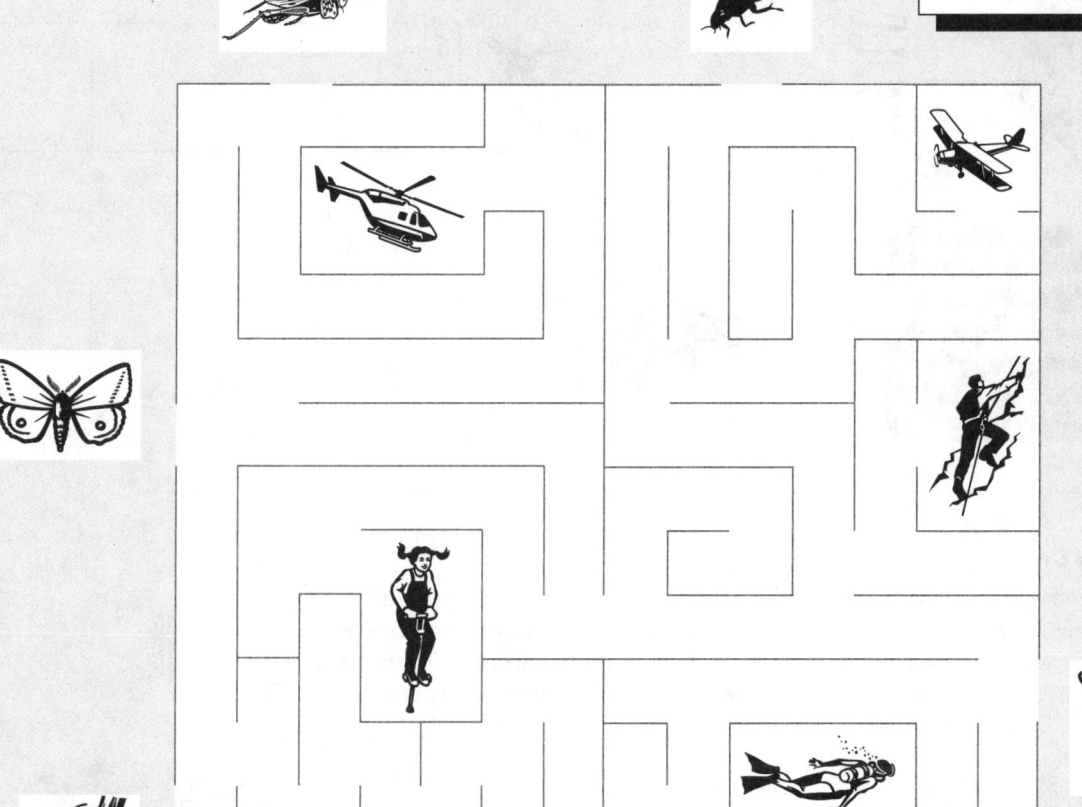

Crossword Challenge

Across

2. thin hollow rods in insect wings
5. part of the reason insects have been so successful
8. what supports the muscles inside an insect's body
10. stage of metamorphosis between the egg and the pupa

Down

1. insect body part between the head and abdomen
3. used for defense or for killing prey
4. an insect with very small back wings
6. insect sense organs
7. an acrobatic insect
8. the first stage of metamorphosis
9. how many legs all insects have

b

ZOOBOOKS ACTIVITIES

Go buggy over these fun insect activities. Use the information in this book to complete the exercises on these four pages. Try these activities on your own or with your family.

Not a Cross Word About Insects

Use the picture clues to complete this puzzle.

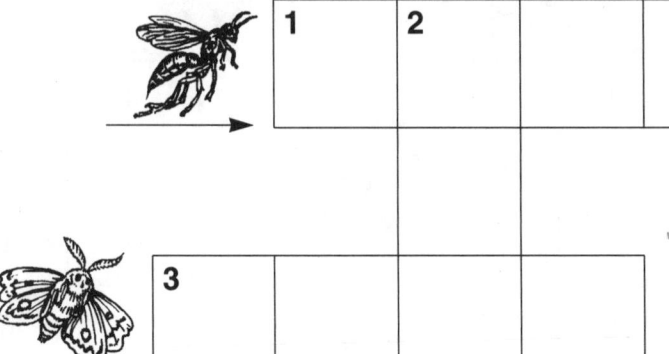

1	2		

3			

Insect Word Search

Hidden in this puzzle are the names of 14 insects (see the list below). Find and circle as many of these insect names as you can. Then try to meet this challenge: Also hiding in this puzzle are the names of 6 tiny animals often mistaken for insects. Find as many of these insect imposters as you can. Circle them in a different color. *To find out what makes an animal an insect, see pages 2 and 3.*

ant
beetle
butterfly
cicada
cricket
dragonfly
fly
katydid
mantis
mosquito
moth
treehopper
walking stick
wasp

```
              A M I T E                                           C R L L V
       B H I Q R T G H J K T          A L           A P         S D V D K N G P R M R
       Q B E E T L E P L R N G          E             R         L X N K D R L S P R K F
       Z V U G F D W T P L N Q S          X         D           F C I C A D A S N D V L A
         T T R H J K Q V C H J L           A N             G N E S D T R K S L N A
         P B T H J L M A N T I S V       F L Y       S T V N S T Y N M R K C R
         R T E V Z B D F H J L N P R T V Z P C R T L N D N S P R K
         F F P R M D V D W A L K I N G S T I C K I K N I G P R M S
           L S N F J R M Y L R N D R S P R L K O P F F D A L E X
             S T L V N L E T N D R S P R L K F E F D B B I
               G Y N E C S H D M R Y H B L D D N S P
               M I L L I P E D E I W R U K R E O F F
                 C A I R L S O A N G C A U
               R R Y M D R Y J N S K O B G R I G
             E R S P T R E E H O P P E R I O R K O F F
             R B C C S C O R P I O N L Y N N N C R L M S N
         J N T J M D M N Q U     A M C   N N F M R C L O N S
         C R I C K E T H D D     A N T     X L N N T H S S P Z
         Z L R F R T N N M         S       Y F N S C T S Q M
       N T N D N T H S B K                 C R M O T H C U L E
       L O B S T E R I S                     S M N Y N S I C T
       D   P C T R                             S S U C   T
     P       D F                                   T H     O
             N                                     I
           D                                       C
         N                                             K
```

a

Insect muscles never get tired, like human muscles do. If an insect could eat enough food, it could keep running or flying for days! People can't do this because they can't supply oxygen to their muscles fast enough. Without oxygen, the muscles get tired. But insects can breathe oxygen directly through many tiny holes, called *spiracles* (spihr-uh-kuhlz), located along the sides of their bodies. They can supply more oxygen to their muscles, and so the muscles don't get tired.

How would you like to climb to the top of Mt. Everest every day, and then climb down again carrying somebody on your back? Leaf-cutter ants are only a fraction of an inch long, but every day they climb 200-foot trees. For their size, that's the same as a human climbing Mt. Everest. Then they carry down pieces of leaf that weigh as much as they do.

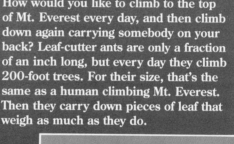

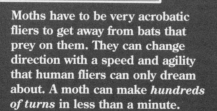

Moths have to be very acrobatic fliers to get away from bats that prey on them. They can change direction with a speed and agility that human fliers can only dream about. A moth can make *hundreds of turns* in less than a minute.

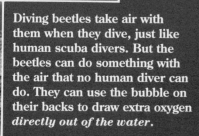

Diving beetles take air with them when they dive, just like human scuba divers. But the beetles can do something with the air that no human diver can do. They can use the bubble on their backs to draw extra oxygen *directly out of the water.*

LEAF-CUTTER ANT

Io Moth

*I*nsect wings are not like the wings of other flying animals. The only other animals that fly are birds and bats. They have wings with bones inside them to keep them stiff. And their wings are covered with feathers or skin. But insect wings are made of two thin layers of exoskeleton. These are held together by thin, hollow rods, called *veins*.

The veins make the wings very strong. Some butterflies can fly thousands of miles on wings that are thinner than a piece of paper. As you will see on these pages, insects use their wings in different ways.

URANIUS MOTH

LUNA MOTH

Some moths have wings so thin that you can almost see through them. A few, like this Luna moth, have clear spots on their wings that you actually can see through.

Scientists call moths and butterflies *lepidoptera* (lep-uh-**dop**-tur-uh). The name means "scaled wings." It fits this group of insects because their wings are covered with thousands of tiny, colored scales. The scales can be arranged in many different ways to give the many different kinds of moths and butterflies their wonderful color patterns.

SATURNID MOTH

Notice how the wings of this beautiful moth overlap. They fit this way so that the front and back wings can move together as one big wing. With so much wing area, butterflies and moths do not have to flap their wings as fast as insects with smaller wings.

Most insects can fold their wings when they are not using them. But some cannot, like this damselfly. Its wings are of a primitive design. The wings of the earliest flying insects may have looked like this.

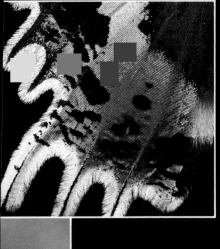

You can see thousands
of colorful little scales
on the wing of this moth.
If you could lift the
scales with your fingers,
you would see the clear,
thin wing underneath.

The front wings on a beetle are
hard and thick. They are not used
for flying. Instead, they protect the
back wings by covering them when
the wings are folded. In order to
fly, the beetle raises its front wings
and releases the back ones.

SCARAB BEETLE

LONG-LEGGED FLY

Insects with small wings may move them
very fast. This fly can beat its wings 200
times per second. Mosquitoes flap their
wings 600 times a second, and tiny
midges can move their wings up and
down *1,000 times every second*!

DAMSELFLY

VEINS OF GRASSHOPPER WING

GRASSHOPPER

Some insects do not have to flap their wings all the
time to stay in the air. When grasshoppers jump,
they unfold their back wings and let the wind carry
them along. Of course, they don't always glide like
this. They can also flap their wings, and sometimes
fly great distances.

Color is found everywhere in the world of insects. Many insects look incredibly beautiful to us. But the insects themselves don't care about beauty. To them, color may be a matter of survival.

Insects use color to keep themselves alive in three different ways. First, they may use it to *camouflage* themselves, making it harder for predators to see them. Second, some insects use *bright colors* as a warning to predators. The colors tell predators that these insects may be poisonous or bad tasting. Third, some insects may *imitate* the bright colors of other insects to make predators *think* they are bad to eat. These insects aren't really poisonous or bad tasting, but the color patterns on their bodies fool predators into thinking they are.

This moth's brilliant colors are a warning that it has a *terrible taste*. It also has a tiny "face" on its back. But nobody is really sure if this also helps protect it. Can you find the face on the moth's back?

TIGER MOTH

LANTERN FLY

BARK MANTIS

Some insects have markings that defend them in more than one way. For example, the lantern fly shown above has an effective camouflage. But it also has markings that can confuse predators. It has real eyes on one end of its body, and false eyes on the other end. A predator that sees it may have trouble telling which way the lantern fly is going.

Now you see it—now you don't! This mantis is so well camouflaged that it seems to disappear before your very eyes.

STINK BUG

BLINDED SPHINX MOTH

BLINDED SPHINX MOTH

Many moths also have *double protection*. First, their front wings may be used to camouflage them. When these wings are folded back, the moth may be hard to see ①. Second, their rear wings may have bright "eyespots" to frighten predators away. To flash its eyespots, a moth simply spreads its front wings ②. The sudden appearance of the "eyes" startles a bird or other predator, so the moth can fly away unharmed.

The amazing color patterns on this beetle are really a sign that says, "Poison—Don't Eat Me!" One bite is enough to make many predators sick.

LEAF BEETLE

This katydid keeps its color hidden until it is needed. When it senses danger, the katydid stands on its head like an acrobat. This reveals markings on the underside of its body that make it look like a wasp.

LEAF BEETLE

The patterns on these beetles look as if an artist painted them with a paintbrush. In a sense, they are painted on, because the colors come from *pigments*—the same kinds of chemicals that make color in paint.

The bright colors on this bug tell predators that it has a *terrible smell*. When attackers come too close, it sprays a foul-smelling chemical into the air.

HORNET MOTH

HOVER FLY

Some insects are "actors." They have "costumes" that fool predators. These insects are usually harmless. They have no sting, no poison, and no bad taste. But their costumes may be enough to make predators think that they are dangerous or not good to eat. For example, the fly at left looks like a honeybee. And the moth at right is imitating a wasp.

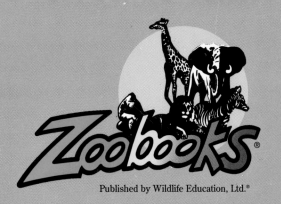

Zoobooks®

Published by Wildlife Education, Ltd.®

ON THE COVER:
A Malaysian Green Preying Mantis

Created and Written by
John Bonnett Wexo

Scientific Consultants
Thomas Eisner, Ph.D.
Schurmann Professor of Biology
Cornell University

Edward J. Maruska
Director
Cincinnati Zoological Gardens

Ronald E. Monroe, Ph.D.
Department of Zoology
San Diego State University

Production Manager
Barbara A. Jones

Editorial Production
Marjorie Shaw
Renee C. Burch

Production Artist
Jim Webb

Circulation
John Lee, Manager
Shirley Patino
Laurie Nichols

Controller
Cecil Kincaid, Jr.

Accounting & Administration
Sandra A. Battah
Paula Dennis
Sally Mercer
James F. Blake II

International Licensing Manager
Debra S. Ives

Sales
Julaine Chattaway, Manager
Rejina Freeman
Carmen Rodriguez

Director of Educational Development
Maria Hagedorn

The California Department of Education
endorses Zoobooks

Photographic Credits
Front Cover: Gerry Ellis (ENP Images); **Inside Front Cover
and Page One:** John Gerlach (Tom Stack & Associates);
Page Two: Top, Kjell B. Sandved; **Left,** L. West (Bruce
Coleman, Inc.); **Right,** Tom McHugh (Photo Researchers);
Page Three: Top Left, Stephen Dalton (Photo Researchers);
Top Right, Andy Crosthwaite (Earth Images); **Bottom Left,**
H. Uible (Photo Researchers); **Bottom Right,** Peter Ward
(Bruce Coleman, Inc.); **Page Four:** John Shaw (Tom Stack &
Associates); **Page Five:** Kjell B. Sandved; **Page Six: Top
Right, Middle Right, and Bottom Right,** Kjell B. Sandved;
Left, Hans Pfletschinger (Peter Arnold, Inc.); **Page Seven:**
Top Left, Michael Fogden (Bruce Coleman, Inc.); **Top Right,**
C. Allan Morgan (Peter Arnold, Inc.); **Bottom Left,** Stephen
Dalton (Photo Researchers); **Bottom Right,** Kjell B. Sandved;
Page Eight: Top Left, John H. Gerard (Bruce Coleman, Inc.);
Top Middle, Kjell B. Sandved; **Top Right,** John H. Gerard
(Bruce Coleman, Inc.); **Second Row, Left,** Gwen Fidler (Tom
Stack & Associates); **Middle,** John Shaw (Tom Stack &
Associates); **Right,** John H. Gerard (Bruce Coleman, Inc.);
Third Row, Left, Kjell B. Sandved; **Middle,** E.R. Degginger
(Bruce Coleman, Inc.); **Right,** Kjell B. Sandved; **Bottom Left,**
Gwen Fidler (Tom Stack & Associates); **Page Nine: Top Left,**
Stephen Dalton (Photo Researchers); **Middle Left,** Rod
Planck (Tom Stack & Associates); **Bottom Left,** Kjell B.
Sandved; **Middle,** Michael Ederegger (Peter Arnold, Inc.);
Top Right, Runk/Schoenberger (Grant Heilman); **Middle
Right,** Kim Taylor (Bruce Coleman, Ltd.); **Bottom Right,**
John Shaw (Tom Stack & Associates); **Page Ten: Top,** Mik
Dakin (Bruce Coleman, Ltd.); **Left,** N. Smythe (Photo
Researchers); **Right,** Dr. Crich (Okapia); **Page Eleven:** Carol
Hughes (Bruce Coleman, Inc.); **Pages Twelve and Thirteen:**
John R. MacGregor (Peter Arnold, Inc.); **Page Fourteen:**
Top Left, Larry West (Bruce Coleman, Inc.); **Bottom Right,**
Bottom Left, Middle Left, and Top Right, Kjell B. Sandved;
Page Fifteen: Top Left, F. Glenn Erwin (Cyr Color Photo
Agency); **Top and Middle Right, Middle, Bottom Left and
Right,** Kjell B. Sandved; **Page Sixteen: Top Right,** Kjell B.
Sandved; **Top Left,** Doug Wechsler; **Middle,** Ian Beames
(Ardea London); **Bottom Left and Middle,** Becky & Gary
Vestal (Earth Images); **Bottom Right,** Kjell B. Sandved;
**Inside Back Cover: Top Right and Left, Middle Right and
Left,** Kjell B. Sandved; **Bottom Right,** Hans Pfletschinger
(Peter Arnold, Inc.); **Bottom Left,** P.H. Ward (Natural Science
Photos).

Art Credits
All paintings by Walter Stuart, with assistance from
Sfona Pelah.

Printed in the U.S.A.

Wildlife Education, Ltd.®
San Diego, California

ISBN 0-937934-22-4

T3-AED-716

90000

9 780937 934227